Banana Boots

Banana Boots

David Fennario

Talonbooks
1998

Copyright © 1998 David Fennario

Published with the assistance of the Canada Council.

Talonbooks
#104—3100 Production Way
Burnaby, British Columbia, Canada V5A 4R4

Typeset in New Aster and printed and bound in Canada by Hignell
Printing Ltd.

First Printing: October 1998

Talonbooks are distributed in Canada by General Distribution
Services, 325 Humber College Blvd., Toronto, Ontario, Canada
M9W 7C3; Tel.:(416) 213-1919; Fax:(416) 213-1917.
Talonbooks are distributed in the U.S.A. by General Distribution
Services Inc., 85 Rock River Drive, Suite 202, Buffalo, New York,
U.S.A. 14207-2170; Tel.:1-800-805-1083; Fax:1-800-481-6207.

Canadian Cataloguing in Publication Data

Fennario, David, 1947-
Banana Boots

A play.
ISBN 0-88922-396-3

I. Title.
PS8561.E54B36 1998   C812'.54   C98-910716-7
PR9199.3.F45B35 1998

to the members of the Felon's Club
in the Falls Road

Banana Boots was first produced in 1994 at the Annex Theatre in Toronto, Ontario, by Mixed Company and directed by Simon Malbogat.

Banana Boots

AUTHOR enters on stage. He sits down and picks up a book from the table.

AUTHOR:
I'm going to read from the first act. The party scene. French and English on their back balcony in Verdun-Pointe Saint-Charles. People been drinking, getting pissed. Paquette goes over to Muriel who doesn't want to dance with him, so he starts dancing with his teenage daughter, Diane. He grabs her ass. She pushes him away and runs down the stairs, down the alleyway. Her mother, Cécile, calls out for her.

AUTHOR starts reading from the text of "Balconville."

CÉCILE:
Diane. Diane.

PAQUETTE:
Who wants to dance, hey?

PAQUETTE heads towards MURIEL.

MURIEL:
Get lost. Beat it.

MURIEL pushes PAQUETTE.

PAQUETTE:
Quoi?

MURIEL:
Ya make me sick.

PAQUETTE:
Hey, parle-moi en français, heh?
Parle-moi en français.

MURIEL:
Go on. Hit me, hit me, try it.

PAQUETTE:
Maudits anglais. How come I got to
speak English, heh? How come?

MURIEL:
'Cause you're stupid.

PAQUETTE:
Maudits anglais. Throw them all out.
Toute la gang. On est au Québec, on
est chez nous.

MURIEL:
> I was born here too, ya big mouth
> Frenchman.

PAQUETTE:
> But it's our turn now, heh? Our turn.
> And h'Ottawa can kiss my Pepsi h'ass.

MURIEL:
> Ferme ta gueule, toi.

THIBAULT:
> Fuck the Queen!

MURIEL:
> Fuck Lévesque!

> *MURIEL goes back into the house.*
> *PAQUETTE knocks over one of*
> *CÉCILE's plants.*

CÉCILE:
> Claude, fais attention à mes plantes,
> Claude.

> *PAQUETTE picks up one of her plants*
> *and throws it over the railing.*

PAQUETTE:
> Tiens, ta câlice de plante.

> *CÉCILE runs into the house crying.*

PAQUETTE:
It's crying time again, heh, crying
time.

*PAQUETTE opens a beer and gives some
to his friend, the grocery boy,
THIBAULT.*

THIBAULT:
Me, I don't hate the English. I just
don't like them, that's all.

PAQUETTE:
Maudits anglais!

THIBAULT:
They got funny heads, square heads.

*PAQUETTE to TOM, the young teenage
boy.*

PAQUETTE:
Hey toi, hey you. Think maybe you
got a chance, heh? No more. That's
the one good thing now. We're all the
same now, heh, all equal. Nobody's
gotta chance. Nobody!

THIBAULT:
Fuck the Queen!

PAQUETTE:
Maybe you got dreams, heh. Me too. I
had dreams. Thibault too, he got
dreams.

THIBAULT:
Oui, me too.

PAQUETTE:
If you know what I know, you'd go jump in that river right now, tonight.

THIBAULT:
Oui, tonight, the river, no joke, that, heh?

> *PAQUETTE gives THIBAULT a drunken hug.*

PAQUETTE:
Thibault, you're a bum. A bum and a drunk.

THIBAULT:
Oui, a bum.

PAQUETTE:
You know what? Me, I work all my life. All my life.

THIBAULT:
That's too bad.

PAQUETTE:
When I was young, I was going to do this and that, but the job, the fucking job, it took my life away. What can you do? Everybody says, what can you do? That's the way it goes.

THIBAULT:
That's the way it goes.

PAQUETTE:
You get h'old, ugly and you die and that's all.

THIBAULT:
That's all.

PAQUETTE:
I try, but it don't help. No matter what you do.

> *TOM exits down the stairs and PAQUETTE yells after him.*

PAQUETTE:
No matter what you do!

THIBAULT:
Heh, so what. That's what I say. So what.

PAQUETTE:
Maudits anglais.

THIBAULT:
So what.

AUTHOR:

Balconville. It was my big hit. Took me a lot of places I never expected to see. Paid my rent for three years. Some people got a house out of it; I got a Toyota. Not bad, I'm not complaining, it was a good ride while it lasted. Sort of like being on a roller coaster that suddenly stops...but you keep going!

All the characters in the play are based on people I grew up with: my mother, my father, my sisters, my brothers and me, very much like the young boy Tom in the play who has some vague idea of becoming a writer or something, somewhere, sometime, some place.

I was the second kid in a family of eight, living on the avenues in Verdun in what was called a four-and-a-half room flat. Cold in the winter like an ice box. Hot in the summer like an oven. Everybody stayed out on their balconies. Hundreds of balconies.

Thousands of balconies. Millions of balconies. A galaxy of balconies. "Where you going this summer?" "Balconville." "Yeah, Miami Bench."

We spent all summer on the streets. The parents out on their balconies and the kids down on the sidewalks playing "Red Rover, Red Rover, Calling Over," "Three Chase the Bunch," "Standall," "Mother, Mother, May I Go Cross the River to Get the Golden Slipper?"

And the girls singing songs like "Hey, hey, hey, did ya hear the news today? Mary's having a baby—and Johnny's going crazy—wrap it up in tissue paper—throw it down an incinerator—how many floors did it fall? One-two-three-four-five-six-seven—all good children go to heaven. When they're bad they go below one-two-three-four-five-six-seven."

And it's getting dark, time to go home, with Mrs. Cleary on her front balcony three floors up— "Dann-nneeee Boy—Yoo hoo, Dann-nneeeeee-eee"

"On the mountain stands a lady—who she is I do not know—all she wants is gold and silver—all she likes is nice young boys."

"I'm gonna kick your goddamn ass, Danny boy!"

Lots of kids around, that's for sure. Diapers on all the washlines and down the avenues, back in the fifties at the peak of the baby boom. My Ma walking down Second Avenue—holding me by one hand, Virginia by the other, pushing Janice in the carriage, with my older sister Peggy Ann carrying the groceries. We pass by Mrs. Cleary sitting on her front steps.

"What's wrong Marge?"

"Ah, that son of a bitch got me pregnant again!"

Love in Verdun. 911.

My parents used to have real fights when I was younger—ashtrays, radios, toasters flipping down the hallways, alarm clocks exploding against the wall. Later they just stopped talking to each other. "Virginia, tell your father his supper's in the oven."

The fights were always over the same thing. Either my father was too cheap or too cold...cold, cold heart. Sad, sad songs by Hank Williams, Hank Snow, Webb Pierce. Songs like "Don't sell Daddy any more whiskey, I know it will take him away." It had a real baby crying in the background. "Don't sell Daddy—wawwwwh—any more whiskey—wawwwwwwh—I know it will take him away—wawwwwwwwwwwwwwwwwwwh!"

"Jesus Christ, father. It's your turn to feed the kid!"

And, when we weren't fighting with each other, we were fighting with the French.

They were moving into what we called "our neighbourhood," coming off the farms after the Second World War, and we didn't exactly welcome them with a 'bienvenue.'

"Va-t-en chez vous, toi." That was the first French I learned. "Fuck you, get on your own side of the street!" That was the first English they learned. "Maudit Bloke," "Peasoup," "Tête carrée," "Pepper."

Not only were we divided into French and English, but there was also something called Protestant and Catholic.

"Catholic, Catholic, ring the bell, Protestant, Protestant, go to hell."

I remember my best friend Danny Casey with the ears, coming home from his first day in school telling me "You're going to hell, 'cause you're a Protestant." But it didn't mean much to me 'cause my family never really went to church. My Ma used to send us off to Sunday School on Sunday morning, because it was the only chance she had to get laid.

But religion was a big thing in those days and I'm five years old and of course I believe in God 'cause they told me to. But I had some pretty confused ideas about who He might be, especially after I was told to memorize *The Lord's Prayer*. "Our Father, Who Art in Heaven?"

Well, my older sister Peggy Anne with the freckles explained to me that heaven was somewhere up there above the diapers on the clotheslines.

But our father wasn't up there. Our father came home every day from painting houses, walking down the hallway, stinking of varsol. Was he God?

"No," my sister Peggy Anne said, "God is not our father, they just call him Our Father."

"But, why do they call him 'our father'?" It didn't make sense.

But I finally figured it out. The Lord's Prayer? God must be the landlord. He's the only person I knew who had all the power and the glory, showing up once a month on our front balcony like he just fell out of the sky, this silhouette behind the curtain. And my Ma would say: "Peggy Anne, put Virginia and Janice in the back room," 'cause we were only allowed two kids in our lease. And then she'd head down the hallway towards that silhouette on the curtain, and, "Hello, Mister Gibeau," she'd say in a little girl voice that she only used on bill collectors and landlords.

Old Gibeau with the Maurice Duplessis mustache.

It was Duplessis' Quebec: repressed, depressed, oppressed and compressed. It was in a fucking box. I mean, the guy wouldn't even let us eat margarine. We had to have it smuggled in from Hawkesbury, Ontario, back in what Mordecai Richler calls "The good old days." But the Québécois refer to that period in their history as "La Grande Noirceur," the Great Darkness. Back when the blacks were shining the shoes, the Chinese were doing the laundry, the Joes were doing the Joe jobs, everybody working for Westmount away up there on the mountain where a handful of filthy rich Anglos owned and controlled not only Quebec but most of Canada. God save our gracious Queen, right up 'til Duplessis died. He actually died, we couldn't believe it, in 1959 when we were finally allowed to enter into the 20th century.

I didn't have any dreams or ambitions back then. I didn't have any plans for myself. People in Verdun don't have plans. Things just happen to them. I mean. I knew vaguely there was a job ahead of me somewhere and that I would probably get married and have kids 'cause that seemed to happen to everybody else, and I was on my way to becoming everyone else when, I wrote a poem.

It happened to me during a geometry class when I was fourteen. I was thinking about a movie I had seen on TV the night before. I don't remember the movie but I remember trying to put my feelings down on paper and it came out in rhyme.

"Hey Gary," I said, turning to the guy sitting next to me, "Hey Gary, I think I wrote a poem."

"What?.... What?"

People in Verdun don't write poetry; they go to movies, watch TV or tell jokes but writing is something they make you do in school.

"What are you doing writing that stuff?" my mother would say, "Won't get you a job."

And when I told my Guidance teacher I was interested in writing, he said, "What do you mean? You're in Science 2, go get measured for a shovel right now!"

Hey, but I fooled them all by becoming a famous Canadian playwright. 'Course I didn't plan it; it just sort of happened to me.

You see, I showed a journal I was keeping to my English teacher, Sally Nelson in Dawson College, and she liked it and had it published by the English Department. Then Maurice Podbrey, who happened to be the artistic director of one of the largest theatres in Quebec, read it and asked me if I wanted to write a play. At the time I thought plays were something people wrote before they invented television, but anyhow I wrote one, and it was *On the Job*. Then *Nothing to Lose*. Then *Toronto*. Then *Balconville*.

"Canada's First Bilingual Play." "High School Drop-Out Has a Sudden Success." "Face In the Crowd Has Story Too."

All very strange. I remember walking off the 107 bus in Verdun, reading in the newspaper that David Fennario was going to Europe. Hey, David Fennario is going to Europe. Hey, that's me.

Everyone was thrilled by the success of *Balconville,* and so was I, up to a certain point. But I found a lot of it confusing 'cause it wasn't as if I had said, hey Dave, you're gonna write a big fucking hit and make a shit load of money. But I did write a big fucking hit and it was making a shit load of money. But I couldn't help but feel that all of this wasn't really happening to me, it was happening to…David Fennario.

In my interviews, I still defined myself as a socialist active in Verdun-Pointe Saint-Charles in the fight for tenant's rights and rights for welfare recipients, telling everyone, hey, don't worry, it's still the same old

Dave. But I was beginning to change into who I was supposed to be, allowing the success to pull me away, up and up and up and up so high I could hardly see where I came from anymore. I figured I knew what I was doing, I thought I knew what was happening, but I was just along for the ride.

People warned me what was happening, but I figured I could always go back home anytime I wanted to. Sometime. Maybe. Later. After I finished my ride.

The British tour of *Balconville*, sponsored by the Department of External Affairs, had us booked for Bath, or Baa-th as they say, pretty as a postcard, then London and the Old Vic where Sir Laurence Olivier once walked the boards, and then Belfast of all places and who knows why. Well, I suppose the Department of External Affairs knows why, but mostly because Belfast was ready to take anyone stupid enough to go there. I mean, I suppose most of us are aware of what's going on in Northern Ireland. Hardly a week goes by without something or someone getting blown up, banana boots and all.

"But not to worry," our British tour director Robert Perceval said, "It's all been highly exaggerated by the media. I assure you that we'll arrive there and you'll hardly notice a thing."

Well, we started noticing things soon as we land in Ireland, right, and we have to go through another security check, after the flight? Then they put us on board a bus to our hotel and I am sitting next to Steven Hawkins who did the lights and Steven's already figured out how he is going to handle Belfast. He's got a forty-ouncer of Bushmill's taped to him, like a fucking transfusion bottle.

"Hey Dave," he says, "I've got relatives in Belfast. It's a scar-rrr-ry place."

But you know people seemed friendly enough and it all looked the way it's supposed to look outside the bus windows on our way to Belfast.

You know all green and luscious like the Ireland that your uncle sings about when he gets pissed at about two in the morning. "Oh Danny Boy," with all the leprechauns hopping around with the fucking hobbits and we're thinking, gee, maybe we'll have fun here. When all of a sudden things start getting less green and more gray and grittier and grimier and greasier as we headed into what's been called the worst slums of Western Europe, going deeper and deeper until we finally reach our destination.

The Hotel Europa, the pride of Ulster, totally surrounded by a twelve foot brick wall, tastefully topped with barbed wire, a security check point box and a firm-but-friendly staff who inform us that the first thing on the agenda is a bomb drill!

There the Hotel Manager comes out into the lobby, this big Mick with a boozy nose and he says:

"ONE: Not to worry because the Hotel Europa hasn't been bombed in over a year.

TWO: But in case of a blast, please follow the instructions given to you by our firm-but-friendly staff, to the letter.

THREE: We prefer that you drink upstairs in our bar on the second floor, but if you insist on going out—and we recommend that you don't go outside—please go over to the Duke Of Gloucester Pub. We wouldn't want you to turn any wrong corners. And,

FOUR: and listen carefully. If ya happen to be outside—and again we recommend that ya don't go outside—but if you happen to be outside and you hear a shot, don't run!"

"Hey, Robert, hey Perceval, we're starting to notice things here!"

And all the Anglophones in the cast start going into a state of denial, "No—no, this is not happening—anyone got the Equity number?" And all the Francophones start getting this hunkered down, dogged look that comes from two hundred years of saying "No, no, no, no, we don't speak the good English, hey Robert, Hey, Perceval, nous voulons le danger pay!"

You see, in Quebec we understand that sometimes people get blown up, but we want to get paid for it. Makes you feel a whole lot better when you're in the hospital bed, resting in pieces, knowing that at least you make a few extra bucks.

I leave them arguing down there about danger pay 'cause I want to check out the bar on the second floor. And it sort of looks like any kind of bar anywhere except for these red lights that make everybody's face look kind of sinister. Then I realize, it's not the lights, the faces are sinister.

That's when I start thinking about that name in my notebook that Big George O'Brien gave me. He's a guy I grew up with on the avenues, in Verdun. A member of the Comité de Solidarité de Québec-Irlande. I didn't think much of it at the time. Big George just said, "Hey Dave, if you're going to Belfast. why don't you give this guy, Danny Moran, a ring and he'll show ya the town." Now I'm beginning to wonder what he meant by that. 'Cause I don't know who this guy Danny Moran is, but I'm pretty sure if he knows Big George O'Brien he's not some kind of a boy scout. 'Cause George is an active supporter of the IRA.

So chickenshit me, I go up to my room, take out that notebook and I'm about to rip out that page, when I start thinking about this guy Danny Moran that I'm never going to meet 'cause I don't want to get involved. But then I'm thinking, oh come on, you've been doing too much of that lately.

So I picked up the phone, when suddenly it hits me: the phone, this phone, maybe all the phones in Hotel Europa, they must be bugged right? Especially here in room 202 where the walls talk back at you.

So I decided I'm gonna go outside and phone.

Did you ever do something brave, 'cause you're stupid? But I figure, hey, it can't be any worse out there than it was during the October Crisis in 1970 when they had tanks all over the streets of Montreal.

So I go downstairs in the lobby and I make it past the Bell Captain who sort of looks like Wimpey. Then the receptionist who looks like Sweet Pea, and the guy in the security box who sort of looks like Bluto!

You see, the guy who invented Popeye was from Belfast, and I can see where he got his faces—Wimpey, Sweet Pea and Bluto watching me go out of the hotel—where the fuck is he going?

So I get outside the hotel next to the twelve foot brick wall, topped with barbed wire. And it's quiet. Too quiet. Then around that corner comes an armoured car with guns sticking out the sides—a Belfast version of a cop car—then around the corner comes a British soldier doing the Belfast walk.

And I tell myself, okay Dave, if you hear a shot, don't run. But I'm walking pretty fast over to the nearest telephone booth and it's busted. And I'm walking even faster over to the next one, and it's busted. And I'm just about to start running when I tell myself—hold it, Dave, better think about this. That's when I heard something really strange.

Ya see, I got this tune that always comes into my head whenever I get really spooked. It's something I picked up from some cartoon movie when I was a kid, that epitomized for me the very essence of Evil. It's a tune I can never recall. I tell myself I'm gonna remember it the next time, but I can't remember it now. But there I was in Belfast and this guy walks by wearing a big pair of banana boots with the toes curled up, and he's singing it!

Well, fuck the wire tap, I go back to the hotel, pick up the phone and "Allo?" It's Danny's wife Kathleen. "Danny!" And hi, no it's not Big George O'Brien from Montreal; it's Little Dave Fennario from Montreal and oh, "Hi Dave—got any messages for me?"

"Well no, Danny, no."

"Oh, oh, okay, Dave, look I'll be around tomorrow to pick ye up in a cab."

"Uh, that's okay, Danny, I mean, I can get my own cab." And I'm thinking, gee this guy is friendly, maybe too friendly.

So I decide I want to talk to Jean Archambault about all this, even though Jean hardly ever says anything to anybody about anything. But I always like to know how Jean feels about things. So I go down to the bar on the second floor and Jean says, "Well, you'll see what happens when it happens." And then Steven Hawkins who said, "You did what?"

But the next morning, ya know, the sun is shining and the place sort of looks like a Holiday Inn, except for the bars on the windows. So, I go down to the lobby to the Bell Captain who looks like Wimpey and tell him I want a cab. When he asked me where, I tell him 52 Broadway.

"52 Broadway?"

"Yeah."

"That's in the Falls, sir."

"Yeah?"

"The Falls Road, sir."

"Okay."

"One moment, sir," he says and then he goes over to this group of taxi drivers standing near the lobby door and I hear him say "Falls Road," and they all turn around and look at me. Then this guy with a pickle for a nose comes over and says, "Where ya going?"

"52 Broadway."

"52 Broadway?"

"Yeah!"

"That's in the Falls."

"Yeah."

"The Falls Road."

"Yeah, I know!"

Okay I'm a bit slow, right, but I'm beginning to figure out that maybe taking a cab from the Hotel Europa to the Falls Road is a bit unusual? So I'm sitting in the back seat of this guy's cab and he's checking me out in the mirror asking me what I'm doing in Belfast, I figure I'll tell him I'm visiting relatives— vvvvrrrrooooommmm—he takes off like a fucking rocket —and eekk—he's turning, he's going through red lights—errkk—he pulls up in front of

52 Broadway. And I get out automatically reaching for my wallet but the guy takes off on me. Never happened to me before where a taxi driver took off without getting paid. Ever happened to you? So like an asshole I start running after him waving my wallet, yelling, "Come back, come back." And all these guys are at the window of 52 Broadway watching me chasing after this guy, waving my wallet, "Come back! Come back!"

First impressions, right?

So, Danny Moran comes out on the sidewalk, he sort of looks like one of the O'Neills off the avenues, big potatohead with blue eyes, and "Hey, Danny," I said, "You were there at the window, what did you think of that performance there, Bluto behind the wheel?"

"Well Dave," he says, "that was a Protestant taxi driver. You got to take a Catholic cab into the Falls. I tried to tell ya on the phone, Dave."

You see, what you got to understand about the Falls Road is

that there's no buses or cars, and the only way to get around is in the co-op taxi cabs that Danny helped organize. Those big London boxes that they send over to Belfast when they break down, and those guys fix them up and drive them around the Falls.

And I got into one with Danny and we're driving over to his place in the Falls where I get to meet his wife Kathleen with the red hair, and I don't know how many kids with red hair, the red hair and the red hair. And there's Pope John the twenty-third on the wall over there, and there's Elvis with sort of a halo around his head, and I think I see a Kennedy on a shelf somewhere. And here's the front room, there's the back room and the hallway, just like in Verdun, ya know, the decor, the ambiance or whatever the fuck you want to call it. It's all there, and even the family dynamics seem familiar with the older daughter yelling 'cause she wants to go out and Danny yelling 'cause he doesn't want her to go out and Kathleen yelling "Let her go out, ya son of a bitch—good to have ye here, Dave."

"Who you calling a son of a bitch, ya bitch—meet ye in the living room, Dave."

So I go in there and say hi to Elvis and I can't help but listen to all the screaming that's going on between Danny and his older daughter and Kathleen who sounds just like my mother and all those other mothers in Verdun, screaming 'cause they don't want to give up and go under and become what they're supposed to become. Second-class citizens with no hope for themselves and their kids, and why can't the older daughter go out and try to find a little love?

"But I want ya back by eleven o'clock, ya hear me?" said Danny. Then he comes into the living room smiling, pours me a shot of Bushmill's, leans over and says, "So, ya got a message for me, Dave?"

"No, Danny, no messages. I'm just here to do a show."

"You're just here to do a show?"

"Yeah."

Then I start telling him what *Balconville* is about but after a while I realize he's not really listening, 'cause I'm not there with a message, right? So he's almost yawning as we sit there with the mashed potatoes and pork chops on the table and big bottle of Bushmill's and I look around and hey it's just me and Danny sitting in there. Where is everybody else? So I get up from the chair, telling Danny I'm going to the can and there's Kathleen and I don't know how many kids all in the kitchen eating french fries so me and the old man can have pork chops together?

So I get on the phone and I order the largest all dressed pizza I can find and I won't bother you with the details of getting an all dressed pizza delivered in Belfast, but I got one. Kind of burnt on the outside with bloodstains and a couple of bullet holes.

And woo-oo all the kids took a piece and then I held one out to Danny, then to Kathleen, the older daughter and the neighbour from next door who wanted to meet the famous Canadian playwright, Margaret. And I'm sort of talking but all she's doing is just staring and kind of twitching her foot at me. Always a good sign when they twitch their foot at you, according to the Verdun sex manual. And I'm thinking, well, shouldn't be too hard to sneak her past the security check point box, the Bell Captain who looks like Wimpey, and all those British spies on the second floor?

Hey, so I invite Margaret and everybody else to come to the opening of my play that Thursday. And when Kathleen asked where it's happening I say, "The Grand Opera House."

"The Grand Opera House," says Danny with a question in his voice. "Well, that's grand, Dave." Then he looks at Kathleen who's ten times tougher than he is and she looks at Danny and he's a hundred times tougher than I am, and she said, "Danny, I'm going!"

Well, I wasn't sure what that was all about and I wasn't sure if I wanted to know so I just took another shot and listened to what Danny was up to.

He told me he was working with a community group and they were actually in the process of doing a show himself. A community play called "Ireland Live On." The story of the Irish struggle against British imperialism over the last eight hundred years. As Danny said, the only struggle longer than the Irish was the women's struggle, and he ought to know about that, 'cause it sure was happening in his house.

So I tell him, yeah sure, I'd like to take in a rehearsal over at the Felon's Club, and saying goodbye to everyone, especially Margaret. I get into the cab with Danny and we're driving along when he said, "Ya know Dave, I think Margaret likes ya."

"A-huh."

"I think she likes ya a lot."

"A-huh."

"Ya know, her old man is doing ten years in jail!"

"Huh."

"Well Dave, the IRA have a policy on wives. Anybody caught screwing them while they're in jail, get kneecapped!"

"Huh?"

"Yeah, ya know, they sort of bend your leg over a curb, and jump on it!"

"Oh...hmmmm."

Anyhow, so we pulled up in front of the Felon's Club where you have to be an ex-con in order to be a member, which includes just about everybody in the Falls Road over the age of three. Danny himself had done five years as a suspected terrorist.

'Terrorist' defined like this: You see, if you're a big country like the United States, Great Britain or Canada, and you go into a small country and you start shooting people, you're a peace keeper. But if you live in one of those small countries and start shooting back— oouuh—you're a terrorist.

And like all the other Republican spots in Belfast, the Felon's Club is completely covered with wire mesh

from the roof down on all sides right
to the sidewalk. And the sidewalk
itself has got boulders cemented in,
so you can't park a car with a bomb
in it too close to the wall. And you go
around to the front gate all festooned
with barbed wire, push the electric
buzzer and this camera turns on ya
and—"Oh, aye, it's Danny Moran and
the famous Canadian Playwright."

And we get inside and the group is
already up on the floor in rehearsal
doing a scene from "Ireland Live On."
It concerns a period in Irish history
known as 'The Black Forties,' when
the potatoes went bad. And in the
space of four years, between 1847
and 1852, a million-and-a-half people
starved to death and another million
emigrated—forced off their land by
British troops, just in case you're
wondering why the Irish are not too
fond of the Union Jack, known over
there as 'The Butcher's Apron.'

I knew a bit about this period of
Irish history because some of those
immigrants came over to Canada. In
the spring of 1847 a hundred

thousand of them came up the Saint Lawrence River in what they called 'coffin ships.' Six thousand of them died in quarantine on Grosse Ile near Quebec City and another six thousand died in Montreal and were buried in a common grave in Pointe Saint-Charles, where I grew up. Shoved into a hole like garbage by the City Fathers.

Now there I was in Ireland listening to these people in the Falls Road tell that story and they were doing it well, telling the history of their community, by themselves, for themselves, with all of it happening right there for them with no distances and no divisions. Not like my play, *Balconville*, stuck up on a stage, over and beyond anything the audience might want to do about the situation they were living in. No, this play was right there being used by them like a weapon.

I didn't know that the theatre could be used that way 'cause, believe it or not, I had never seen a community play before. You know, usually people in theatre start off in community halls and then work their way up to the Main Stage. But I had started off on the Main Stage and have been working my way down ever since. And I've been doing pretty good at it lately, too.

So after the rehearsals finished, I went to the bar with the cast and I wanted to talk to them about community theatre but they were more interested in listening to me because I was a "for real" playwright doing "for real" theatre. So I started telling them what *Balconville* was about, you know, the conflict between the French and English and the need for solidarity. But somehow as I was talking I realized I sounded like I was doing an interview and everything I was saying sounded false even though I was saying the right things. So, I shut up and said, "Look why doesn't everyone come to the opening of my show?" And everybody was into it, right? Except for this guy who looked like James Cagney with a bad hangover and he says, "Why the fuck

would I want to go to the Grand
Opera House?"

Well, I knew where that was
coming from, right? But it still pissed
me off, I mean, it wasn't as if I
planned to do a show there. It just
happened to me; just like I didn't plan
to become famous. I just happened to
be the right guy at the right time
writing the right stuff and BOOM—
right to the top. So—what was I
supposed to do? Jump?

Back at the hotel room, I'm sitting
at the edge of the bed telling myself,
"Well, fuck it, Dave, why should I
worry about what they think? I got
nothing to prove. I mean, I know who
I am, I think, sitting there looking at
myself in the mirror, seeing myself
sitting there in the Hotel Europa....
What the fuck am I doing here?"

And suddenly I'm remembering
something someone once said to me
in passing, a single comment made
by a stranger with a knowing face,
telling me that "You're going to be
used in ways you'll probably never
understand."

Is this what he meant?

So I poured myself a shot of Bushmill's when the phone rang and it was Rosemary from Bath, a publicity person I got to know when I was there doing my show. She drove me around to all the interviews in her red Jaguar convertible, with her gorgeous blonde hair blowing in the wind. So strange to hear her chirpy British voice on the line telling me that she already reserved a seat for me on the London to Bath train where we planned to have supper together.

"I'm so looking forward to seeing you again, David," she said.

She liked me, ya know, she really did. But somehow her accent on the phone was making me paranoid. I mean, I was doing the Belfast Walk just listening to the way she enunciated her words, perfectly pronounced, even though she was supposed to be having an emotional moment.

Trained; they're all trained from birth, those fucking Brits and their fucking Empire.

Hey, you think it's all gone? You think it's all Just History? Well, take a look at this. (*Pulls out a twenty dollar bill*) She's still on the money where it counts, eh?

Proper enunciation always reminds me of Miss McDowell, a teacher I had back in Grade Nine when Winston Churchill was still alive. A regular churchgoer and Sunday School teacher. A Presbyterian whose mission in life was to get us to pronounce our words properly. As you can imagine we didn't get along too well because I've always had trouble with my T's, along with the rest of Verdun, And I got this slouch. "Sit up, David."

I had her for History using this book (*holds up book*) *Building the Canadian Nation*. Chapter one: "First Steps Towards Democracy and Self-Government In A Free Empire."

Listen to this: "Canada is unique amongst American countries in the way in which it grew to Nationhood. Every other American country in the Western Hemisphere broke away from the Empire to which it belonged and gained self-government by Revolution. In contrast with this, Canada stayed with the British Empire and grew to Nationhood step-by-step, in a peaceful manner."

Don't you get the feeling that they left something out? I bet they're still teaching a variation of this in high schools today. Canada the Good. Try telling that to Quebec, the Mohawks or Somalia.

So, Miss McDowell asks for volunteers in the class to do a talk on Lord Durham's Report on the Rebellion of 1837. And I got my hand up 'cause History's always been my favourite subject. Ever since I asked my father where the sidewalks came from. So, I got my hand up and Miss McDowell is looking around me, looking through me, doesn't want to take me 'cause even if I do it right it's wrong, 'cause I got this slouch and I can't pronounce my T's properly either, so, "Very well, David, but sit up."

I started going through the books and this is what Lord Durham had to say in his Report on the Rebellion of 1837 in Quebec. "The Canadiens," he said, "as a people have no history and no literature. They are hopelessly inferior. A race of men habituated to incessant labour by a rude and unskilled agriculture. An uninstructed, inactive, unprogressive people." Sounds like Preston Manning.

I'm a kid, right? I'm really young and my older sister Peggy Anne is taking me out to a picnic in Saint-Willibrord's Park. We got egg sandwiches my mother made and a big bottle of Kik Cola for a dime. It was my mother's way of getting rid of us so she could drink her quart of beer in peace. And we're there sitting on our blanket and everybody else is sitting on their blankets, all doing the same thing when suddenly a gang of teenagers go running by us and start kicking the people a few feet away from us, throwing their food around and chasing them out of the park. It scared me, ya know, and I asked my sister why they did it.

" 'Cause they're French," she said. And I'm really young and I'm thinking, well, what if they thought I was French? And I decided that would be the theme of my talk: What would I think of Lord Durham's Report if I were French?

Miss McDowell seemed more than usually uptight the morning that I was supposed to do my talk in front of the class. Which surprised me, 'cause why should she be nervous when it was me that had to do the talking? But Miss McDowell knew, if I didn't know, that there was more to my slouch than meets the eye.

"Well then, David," she said with a smile—one of those awful smiles that Presbyterians have, from the teeth out. "Are you ready to do your talk?"

"Uh, yes Miss." And I stood up. "Uh."

"Yes?"

"Uh, if I were French...."

"Yes?"....

And I couldn't talk.

I think I had a nightmare that night
about Miss McDowell in the Hotel
Europa, only her face kept changing
into Rosemary's and Rosemary's kept
changing into hers, and we were
trying to make out but over and
above and in-between everything we
were trying to do, there was this
proper enunciation.

"Was-It-Good-For-You?
It-Was-Good-For-Me."

So the next morning I go
downstairs to have breakfast in the
restaurant in the hotel and the whole
cast is there talking about the gunfire
they heard around two in the
morning. So I started talking about
what I was learning about Belfast,
how people were being put in prison
and shot on the streets because they
didn't want to live with 65 percent
unemployment and all those other
things we talk about in *Balconville*,
like the need for solidarity in the face
of a common enemy and I really
think we should speak out for these
people, say something, do
something.... And I look around and

everybody sort of got their heads stuck in their ham and eggs.

So I'm about to sit down, right, a little embarrassed after having had my big moment there in the middle of the restaurant when Robert Perceval, the Tour Director, comes over and says to me in that commanding tone that the British like to use on colonials and other lesser breeds, "Well then, David," he said, "I believe I'm speaking for the whole cast when I say that we're rather concerned about what you might or might not say during our visit in Belfast. It's all right, I suppose, to indulge in a little rhetoric once in a while, but here it is rather a different case, don't you think? After all, we're only in Belfast to do our show."

And I'm nodding, right, 'cause that's what happens to me when I get talked to in the commanding tone that certain Brits like to use on colonials and other lesser breeds, I go into the automatic nod. But I knew he was bullshitting me 'cause I knew that some of the cast would also like to say or do something.

So, "I can understand your concern, Robert," I said, "but I'm afraid we're already taking a stand here whether you like it or not."

"Oh?"

"Yeah. There's that certain line said by the character Thibault in Act One, 'Fuck the Queen'?"

"Oh," he said. "Oh, well, we can always cut."

And that's when I got my nod right.

"Not without my permission."

And, I really didn't want to go to the opening night but I knew my Falls Road gang would be there, so I went. And there in the lobby Steve Hawkins tells me that Jean Archambault, who plays the character of Thibault, wants to see me backstage.

You see, by this time Jean was under pressure from the management and some of the cast to cut the line 'Fuck the Queen.' But Jean, who remembers when being French meant you were a piece of shit, Jean who remembers when being gay meant you were a criminal, doesn't want to cut it unless I say so.

"Ça dépend de toi, Jean," I said, and he looked at me. "Well," he said, "I'll see what happens when it happens."

Then I go back out into the lobby and there's my Falls Road gang, about thirty of them, but I can hardly recognize them 'cause they were all so dolled up. Some of them even looked like they had facelifts, for fuck's sake...and Margaret sure looked good. Too good.

And I'm heading over to them when Robert Perceval cuts me off and says, "David, we can't have these people here."

"Well, I'm not going to tell them to leave."

"David."

"No!"

And I'm pushing my way by him when this security guard about the size of the Eaton's Centre blocks me off and says "Your lot, upstairs!"

And we got a guard in front of us,
a guard in the back, going up the
stairs with my Falls Road gang all
bunched up together into just one big
organism, down this long corridor
into this small gallery overlooking
this huge theatre space, and down
there there's one thousand two
hundred Protestants with carrots up
their asses, and up there it's just me
and my Falls Road gang with a guard
on every door and it finally hits me
why Danny had that question in his
voice when I said, "Hey, let's all go to
the Grand Opera House," 'cause I just
brought them all to a place where
we'll probably all get killed. Not that
anyone looked that worried 'cause
dying is the second worst thing that
can happen to you in Belfast. Living
is the first. Okay, so you might get
shot, but hey, it could be worth it.

So I sit down next to Steven
Hawkins, as far away from Margaret
as I can get, and he's still got that
forty ounce bottle of Bushmill's taped
to him like a fucking transfusion
bottle. And I take a slug and he takes

a slug and we're both wondering if Jean is going to do that line. And poor Jean he's backstage wondering if he's gonna do the line, 'cause he won't know if he's gonna do it 'til maybe it comes out of his mouth automatically.

And the play starts and I take another slug and Steven takes another slug and the closer we get to Jean's big scene the more we're pulling at the bottle and pulling at the bottle with just an inch left with both us tugging on it when I look up and there's Jean leaning on the railing. He opens his mouth, he's opening his mouth....

"F-f-fuck the Queen."

Say it again, Jean.

"Fuck the Queen."

Thanks Jean.

After that the audience sort of relaxed and the Protestants downstairs actually pulled some of the carrots out of their assholes and had a few laughs. But the more noise they made, the more quiet my Falls Road gang became, which disturbed me.

Then the show ends and the cast takes a bow, happy to be in one piece, and we get escorted down from the gallery with a guard in the front and a guard in the back, my Falls Road gang all bunched up in a circle-the-wagons survival mode, and by this time I was getting used to addressing them as if they were just one big organism.

"Hey organism," I said. "Look, I got to go do some interviews but I'll be back in a half hour and I'll meet you over at the Duke of Gloucester pub. Free food, free booze.

"Where?"

"At the Duke of Gloucester. Look Danny, they told me it was safe. I'll meet you there in a half hour."

Half hour later I walk into the pub and I expected to see this feeding frenzy soon as I walked in the door but no, there they were all bunched up in a corner in the circle-the-wagons survival mode and, "Hey Danny," I said. "They told us it was safe."

"Yeah, for them."

It seems the Duke of Gloucester pub was practically a clubhouse for the UDL, the Ulster Defence League, and every one of them is walking around with their badges on, the Red Hand of Ulster, and one of them passes by Kathleen—and something happened that I've never seen before and hope I never see again—craaaccckkk—a blue streak of electricity with Kathleen turning on the guy and me and Danny pushing her and all the rest of the fucking organism towards one of those big old booths they got in those kind of pubs, and I slam the door and yeah I go get some food and then, Kathleen tells me she ain't leaving til she's had a drink, so I go and get some drinks and then Margaret says she wants to see the rooms in the Hotel Europa, and I go and get myself a drink and Danny's on the phone to the Falls Road, and the Protestants are getting restless and that first bottle goes flying and we're out of there—come on come on—out on the sidewalk just as the Falls Road taxi cabs show up and the doors are opening and Danny's yelling—Kathleen, forget the fucking drink!—and the doors are slamming and the last thing I remember as the cabs pull away is Margaret's face looking at me through the window—Sorry.

So the next morning after having given everybody such a good night out, I'm due out on the 403 Flight from Belfast to London. And Danny's waiting outside the Hotel Europa for me with the engine running. It's really running cause he's not supposed to be there. Risking his life again for my convenience, which makes me feel worse than I'm already feeling, and me feeling bad makes him feel worse.

"Hey Dave," he says, "It was a good show. I liked it."

"Yeah, good for who?"

And he checks out my tone of voice and all of a sudden he's laughing. "Hey Dave," he says, "last week I'm at this pub and they got this guy there. Calls himself Bananaboots. A protestant up there wearing a big pair of those shitkickers with the toes

curled right up, and he's making fun
of Paisley and he's making fun of the
Pope. He's got Paisley like this with a
spoon up his arse-hole, he's got the
Pope with a bucket of holy water
blessing the whole audience. And
they're pissing themselves laughing
and I'm pissing myself laughing and I
can't believe I'm laughing cause I'm
supposed to be shooting this guy. Ya
gotta go see him, Dave, before
somebody does shoot him."

And I'm thinking, well yeah,
Bananaboots, well he went and did it.
He put his ass on the line and
brought a few people together. Doing
what I thought *Balconville* could do
once upon a time, before I ended up
being David Fennario, this other
person who talks in quotations as if
he's trying to remember what he is
supposed to believe in. And don't give
me that shit about all this just
happened to you Dave. Because
you've got to do something about
this. You've got to organize your life!

And I'm sitting in Rosemary's
favourite pub in Bath trying to

explain all this to her but it's not what I'm supposed to be saying, ya know? I'm a funny guy and I'm supposed to be making jokes but I'm just going on and on about how unhappy I am doing shows for people who don't care about where I'm coming from. I mean, I'm supposed to be writing shows about the working class for the working class, right? So what am I doing sitting in the Hotel Europa looking at myself in the mirrors? Can you explain that to me?

She doesn't even know where to begin. And I look at her, and she's so beautiful and blonde, one of those blondes that seem to glow from the inside! A very decent person really, and none of this is her fault even though she is part of it. We're all a part of it—but some of us want changes and some of us don't. And Rosemary's doing all right with her Jaguar, her country house and me there to entertain her, sort of 'cause I wasn't really being that funny, and she's waiting 'cause the moment has arrived. And, uh, I've already had four beers and I'm about to order another one when she looks me in the eyes, makes me look at her and, uh, "No," I said.

"Oh..." she said. "Well, goodbye."

And I watched her get up from that table and walk out of the pub with her gorgeous blonde hair heading out that door. And she was gone.

And, I didn't know it at the time. I thought it was just me saying goodbye to Rosemary and Rosemary saying goodbye to me. But it was more than that. Because whether I knew it or not I had just jumped off that ride. Or was I pushed? Did I quit or was I fired?

I really can't say but I do know that what I saw in the Felon's Club inspired me to go back to Pointe Saint-Charles where I got in touch with a community group and together we did my first community play called *Joe Beef, A History of Pointe Saint-Charles*.

Since then I've done most of my stuff with small theatre companies that have a mandate for social change. And it hasn't always been easy as probably some of you out there know, trying to balance a political commitment along with paying the rent. But at least now when I read my name in the newspapers, I know it's me.